Legends of Rock & Roll

Ringo Starr

(Before, During & After the Beatles)

An unauthorized fan tribute

By: James Hoag

Legends of Rock & Roll – Ringo Starr (Before, During and After the Beatles)

"Legends of Rock & Roll – Ringo Starr (Before, During & After the Beatles)" Copyright 2012 James Hoag. All rights reserved. Manufactured in the United States of America. No parts of this book may be reproduced in any form or by any electronic or mechanical means including information storage and retrieval systems without written permission from the publisher. The only exception is for a reviewer. A reviewer may quote brief passages in a review. Published by www.number1project.com Monument Marketing Publishing LTD., 53 Hanover Dr., Orem, Utah 84058

Paperback Edition

Manufactured in the United States of America

Also by James Hoag

Legends of Rock & Roll Volume 1 - The Fifties

Legends of Rock & Roll Volume 2 - The Sixties

Legends of Rock & Roll Volume 3 - The Seventies

Legends of Rock & Roll – The Beatles

Legends of Rock & Roll – Paul McCartney

Legends of Rock & Roll – John Lennon

Legends of Rock & Roll – George Harrison

Legends of Rock & Roll – Neil Diamond

Legends of Rock & Roll – Queen

Legends of Rock & Roll – Eagles

Legends of Country Music – Reba McEntire

Legends of Country Music – Willie Nelson

Legends of Country Music – Johnny Cash

Legends of Country Music – George Jones

Legends of Country Music – Merle Haggard

Legends of Country Music – Garth Brooks

Legends of Rock & Roll – Ringo Starr (Before, During and After the Beatles)

(Available at Amazon.com)

TABLE OF CONTENTS

Table of Contents — 5

Introduction — 7

1-Boyhood — 9

2-A Musical Life Begins — 11

3-Becoming a Beatle — 13

4-Maureen Cox — 16

5-Being a Beatle — 18

6-The Greatest Drummer in the World? — 20

7-The Famous Break-up and Going Solo — 22

8-Getting a Little Help From His Friends — 24

9-Diversity — 26

10-*Goodnight Vienna* — 28

11-*Blast From Your Past* — 30

12-Ring O'Records — 32

13-Barbara Bach — 34

14-Into the Eighties — 36

15-Ringo Starr and His All-Starr Band — 38

16-Fun with the Simpsons — 40

Legends of Rock & Roll – Ringo Starr (Before, During and After the Beatles)

17-The Twenty-First Century	42
18-*Liverpool 8*	44
19-Legacy of Ringo Starr	46
Afterword	48
About the Author	50
Films	51
Selected Discography	53
Studio Albums	53
Live Albums	54
Singles	54

INTRODUCTION

I first heard the Beatles, like most everyone else in the United States, on the radio in early 1964. I had just gotten out of the Air Force, just missed having to go to Vietnam and was studying in college, working on a degree. I would listen to the radio while I studied and remember the Beatles suddenly being played a lot.

In February of 1964, they seemed to take over the airwaves. They performed three shows on the Ed Sullivan Show which was one of the highest rated shows on television. I can remember sitting in the living room with my mother watching the show and thinking, "Here was something new" We, in American had not seen anything like the Beatles before.

Of course, as you watch the Beatles, your attention is drawn to the three guys out front with the guitars. They were obviously the stars of the show. Not everyone noticed the guy in the back beating on the drums, keeping the rhythm going for the rocking songs like "Let Me Hold Your Hand" and "Love Me Do".

John Lennon was called the "smart" Beatle, Paul was the "handsome" or "popular" Beatle and George was known as the "quiet" Beatle. Ringo is the "lovable" Beatle. I did not make this up.

But this book is not really about the Beatles. While you can't discuss the life of Ringo Starr without including the Beatles, my intent here is to concentrate on Ringo the man, as an individual. We'll cover his youth, his years with the Beatles and more importantly, his career after the Beatles.

Ringo Starr may not have been in the spotlight quite as much as the others, but he was an important part of the band. When the Beatles

Legends of Rock & Roll – Ringo Starr (Before, During and After the Beatles)

first organized, they didn't have a drummer. The first time they left England to perform in Germany, they hired Pete Best because they knew they needed a drummer for the band. Later Best was replaced by Ringo and the Beatles as we know them were born.

Ringo was the first non-American drummer to really make a difference in the field. The drum had basically been invented in the United States (at least as a musical instrument). Ringo elevated the instrument so that it was an equal with the other three performers. His drumming style was so unique and original that you could listen to just the drum part of a Beatles song and be able to recognize the song. Something unheard of before Ringo came on the scene. They say that Ringo but the "beat" in Beatles.

In this Legends of Rock & Roll report, I will conclude the four-part mini-series of each of the Beatles by discussing the life and music of Ringo Starr. He has his own story to tell and he had his own music and deserves more recognition than he usually gets.

1-Boyhood

For the first nineteen years of his life, Ringo Starr did not exist. Ringo was born Richard Starkey on July 7, 1940. That would make him the oldest member of the Beatles since John wasn't born until October of the same year and Paul was born in 1942 and George in 1943. Richard was born in an inner city section of Liverpool, England called The Dingle. Americans would call it the suburbs. He lived at 9 Madyrn Street in Liverpool for the first three years of his life.

His parents were Richard Starkey and Elsie Gleave. He was obviously named after his father. Some sources say his Dad worked as a confectioner which as far as I can tell is a seller of confections, or in other words, sweets or candy. Others say he was a baker which could be similar to being a confectioner. Richard, or "Ritchie" as they called him when he was young, was an only child and often lonely. He wished he had brothers or sisters to talk with but never did. Later, he would refer to the other Beatles as his "brothers".

Ritchie's parents broke up when he was three and it was just Ritchie and his mother until he turned eleven. Then his mother met a man named Harry Graves and they started dating. Ritchie liked Graves and encouraged the relationship. Elsie and Harry married when Ritchie was almost 13. The family moved to a new address at 10 Admiral Grove in Liverpool. This was a smaller house than he had come from, but the family got along alright. Graves was the person who got Ritchie interested in music. Ritchie always referred to Graves as his step-ladder.

Ritchie was born left-handed, but when he was a child, his grandmother forced him to learn to write with his right hand. He thus became ambidextrous. His grandmother thought that people who were left handed were under the spell of a witch and she wanted to break him of the spell.

Ritchie was a sickly child. He spent many months in hospital during his growing up years. At the age of six, he experienced a severe case of appendicitis from which complications developed and he actually fell into a ten week coma. After he came out of the coma, while still in the hospital, he attempted to hand a toy to a child in the adjoining bed, fell out of bed himself and received a concussion. When he was 13, he got pleurisy which is an inflammation of the lining of the lungs. It can cause a great deal of pain to just breathe. Ritchie was sent to a sanatorium where he would stay for 2 years.

Ringo said later that one of the highlights to being in the hospital was that occasionally, local bands would roam the hallways and play for the patients. He listened to the different bands and decided that that was what he wanted to do with his life.

Needless to say, these illnesses had a negative effect on his school work. At the age of eight, he could not read or write. A neighbor girl was asked to help him learn. He missed so much school that he was not eligible to take the 11-plus exam that most children took when they reached the age of eleven. Both Paul and George had taken the exam and passed it. This test was used to determine what sort of secondary school the child would attend. Its outcome could influence the career and job possibilities for the rest of his life.

Ritchie attended primary school at St Silas, a Church of England school near where he lived. And he went to secondary school at Dingle Vale Secondary Modern School but he dropped out when he was 15.

Like Paul McCartney, Ritchie was a vegetarian most of his life. Paul was a vegetarian because of ethical reasons, but Richard had had so much sickness as a boy that he discovered being a vegetarian solved most of those problems.

2-A Musical Life Begins

Like many boys his age in the Fifties in England, skiffle was the rage. John Lennon's original group, The Quarrymen was first a skiffle group and then evolved into a rock and roll group. Skiffle originated in the United States, mostly among the black musicians of the south, but had become extremely popular in England in the Fifties. The music is kind of a home-spun music which used homemade instruments and used unlikely objects as instruments, like the washboard.

In England, skiffle was closer to jazz than it was in the United States. The banjo was a big part of a shiffle group as was the guitar. The most famous skiffle group was Lonnie Donegan who had a few hits in the United States including the comedy record "Does Your Chewing Gum Lose Its Flavor (On the Bedpost Overnight)" which was a number five hit in 1961.

Ritchie worked several jobs before coming to music. He worked as a delivery boy for British Rail but had to quit when he failed the medical exam. Next he worked as a barman on a ferry between Liverpool and Wales but was again fired when he came to work drunk. Lastly he worked as a trainee joiner for the engineering firm Henry Hunt & Sons.

Ritchie joined up with a friend of his, Eddie Miles to form the Eddie Clayton Skiffle Group. Miles also worked at Henry Hunt & Sons and the band entertained the workers during lunch hour. This was 1957 and Ritchie was seventeen years old. A couple years later, in 1959, he joined a western group called the Raving Texans. A year later, in 1960, the Raving Texans became Rory Storm and the Hurricanes and they started playing around England in various clubs.

Legends of Rock & Roll – Ringo Starr (Before, During and After the Beatles)

It was while a member of the Hurricanes that he officially took on the name of Ringo Starr. His first name Richard evolved into "Rings" because he was known for wearing several rings on his hands and had picked up the nickname. Then it changed further to Ringo which was easier to say. Starkey became Starr and during their concerts, Ringo would always do a drum solo which came to be known as "Starr Time". In 1959, he made it official and would forever after that be known professionally as Ringo Starr. However, all of the songs for which he gets writing credit show the name of Starkey as the song writer.

Hamburg, Germany was becoming a favorite place for English bands to go and practice their trade. While the Hurricanes were in Hamburg in 1960, Ringo met the rest of the Beatles as they were playing there as well. He liked to hang out with the Beatles when the Hurricanes weren't playing. At this point in time, the Hurricanes were actually more popular than the Beatles were. He even sat in with them on a couple numbers and recorded with them. All this before he became a part of the group.

3-Becoming a Beatle

After returning to the U.K., Ringo had the opportunity to sit in on a session with the other guys, temporarily taking Pete Best's place. Brian Epstein, who had taken over as manager of the Beatles, heard Ringo and decided he would make a better drummer than Best. George Martin, their record producer also did not like Best and asked the guys who they would choose as a new drummer. They picked Ringo because Ringo had played with them and they knew what he could do. So Best was fired and Ringo hired. The rest is history.

Ringo's first appearance with the band was on August 18, 1962. At first, the fans were upset. They picketed the Cavern Club where the group played frequently and held vigils outside of Pete Best's house. They shouted "Pete Best Forever! Ringo Never!" One angry fan even punched George Harrison and gave him a black eye, although the change was not really his fault.

The very first song the Beatles released was "Love Me Do" in 1962. Ringo was still an unknown for the band and they weren't sure what he could do. So, for the first recording of "Love Me Do", they used a session drummer named Andy White and Ringo was relegated to shaking a tambourine. Several tries later, on September 4, 1962, they let Ringo do the drum work and that was the version that was released to the public. There was never any doubt after that that Ringo was meant to be a part of the group.

Ringo plays on every Beatles song during the Sixties that I am aware of. However, there was a time in 1964 when he couldn't tour with them and they had to bring in a substitute drummer. In June, 1964, after having come to American earlier in the year, they were set for an extended tour of Europe, Asia and Australia. On June 3, the day before the tour was to leave, Ringo collapsed during a photo session for the Saturday Evening Post magazine.

He was rushed to the hospital where it was discovered that he had a severe case of tonsillitis and he was running a 102 degree fever. George wanted to delay the tour when they found out Ringo was sick, but their producer George Martin convinced him and the other that they could go on with a replacement drummer until Ringo got better. They asked session drummer Jimmie Nicol who was familiar with the Beatles music.

Nicol was the drummer for the first few days of the tour and on June 11, Ringo was released from the hospital and was able to join the tour in Melbourne, Australia on June 15. Ringo later stated that he was really worried that his replacement might become permanent and he could be out of the band. But, of course, that didn't happen.

I am not aware of any rivalry among the members of the Beatles, at least not at the beginning. It seems that the others liked Ringo and liked his expertise as a drummer. At first Ringo was just the drummer and wasn't spotlighted as an individual that much. As time went on, John and Paul recognized that each of the members of the band should be featured from time to time so that the fans got to know everyone.

John and Paul were the two up front the most. They wrote most of the songs for the group, but at least once per album, they tried to write a song just for Ringo or George. This happened more in the later years of the Beatles, after they had matured a little and the music was more serious.

By 1965, the Beatles were tired of touring. That seems soon to me since they had only been in the spotlight in the United States for about a year and a half. But, they had been performing since 1962 and were weary of singing the same songs over and over. Also, they had grown up a bit. There is a real distinction between the type of music the Beatles sang in their early years and what they wrote and sang later. I used to call the later music, the drug years, but it was more than that. They were maturing as musicians and becoming much more serious about what they were doing.

4-Maureen Cox

In the early Sixties, before they really became famous, the Beatles played The Cavern Club in Liverpool quite often. They could be seen there frequently from 1961 until 1963. Sometime during this period, Ringo met a young hairdresser named Maureen Cox. Maureen was born Mary Cox on August 4, 1946 in Liverpool. She kept the name Mary until about the age of fourteen when she started training as a hairdresser. At this point, she changed it to Maureen and would be known as Maureen for the rest of her life.

Maureen said she had to be really careful being Ringo's girlfriend. The fans did not like the fact that the boys might be seeing girls on a steady basis. Maureen was threatened and actually attacked on occasion by angry female fans that didn't like it that she was dating Ringo. None of the boys were supposed to have "steadies" or girlfriends, while, in fact, all four of them did. John had married Cynthia Powell but no one knew about it.

Ringo had to have his tonsils removed in December of 1964 and Maureen came to Liverpool to nurse him. One thing led to another and they discovered that Maureen was pregnant. On January 20, 1965, Ringo proposed marriage. She said yes and they were married in London just a couple weeks later on February 11, 1965 and Zak Starkey, their first child, was born September 13, 1965. They honeymooned at Prince's Crescent in Hove, England, which is on the south coast of England.

Ringo arranged for Frank Sinatra to sing a re-written version of his famous song "The Lady is a Tramp" just for Maureen. Sinatra had Sammy Cahn, who had written many Sinatra sons, re-write some of the lyrics and personalize them for Maureen. The original song is from

James Hoag

"Babes In Arms" by Rodgers and Hart. One line which Cahn changed goes as follows: "She married Ringo, and she could have had Paul/That's why the lady is a champ" They pressed only a few singles of the song and labeled it as "Apple 1" meaning it was the first record published under the Apple label. Then the master was destroyed and that makes this one of the rarest records on earth.

Maureen and Ringo stayed together ten years, divorcing in 1975. Ringo had not had any brothers or sisters and he didn't want his children to suffer that, so after Zak, Jason was born August 19, 1967 and a daughter, Lee Parkin, was born November 11, 1970. It is said that the marriage was really over in 1970 when the Beatles broke up. It is known that both Ringo and Maureen were having affairs with other people and at one point; Ringo came home to find George Harrison in bed with his wife. They limped along until 1975 when the divorce became final.

Maureen Cox married again after the divorce. Ringo called her two hours after John had been killed to give her the news of John's death. Maureen died of complications from leukemia on December 30, 1994. She was at home at the end, with her four children and second husband and Ringo.

5-BEING A BEATLE

One song that was written for Ringo during this later period was "Yellow Submarine". This was meant to be a children's song and Paul did most of writing, although there was input from John and Donovan (remember "Sunshine Superman"). Paul says he knew when he was writing the song that it was meant for Ringo. "Yellow Submarine" is included on the *Revolver* album. The song went to number one on all the British charts and peaked at number two in the United States in 1966.

Their big album of 1967 was *Sgt. Pepper's Lonely Hearts Club Band* which was a masterpiece. It is recognized by a lot of rock and roll lists as the best album of the rock era including being number one on Rolling Stone magazine's list of the 500 Greatest Albums of All Time. Ringo had a song in Sgt. Peppers which was "With a Little Help From My Friends". The song, written by Lennon and McCartney was for Ringo and he does a great job on it. Although, we don't think of Ringo as a singer, he can sing very well and proves it on this song.

It's interesting to note that the song was written under the working title of "Bad Finger Boogie" before being changed to "With a Little Help from My Friends". This original title was the inspiration for the group Badfinger who had several hits in the early Seventies.

Ringo was famous for providing several titles and ideas for songs which the group wrote and recorded. They became known as "Ringoisms" and were phrases that were just a little bit off. "A Hard Day's Night" was first said by Ringo just in passing and Paul picked up on the phrase and made it a song. "Tomorrow Never Knows", a song from the album *Revolver* is another one, as is "Eight Days a Week"

Paul called these Ringo's malapropisms. A malapropism is a familiar phrase which has one or more of its words changed to something which sounds the same but gives it an entirely different meaning. Ringo was somewhat famous for these and Paul and John used them in several songs.

Ringo felt left out when it came to songwriting. He wasn't really a songwriter, but he wanted to contribute. One line which he contributed to the song "Eleanor Rigby" was "darning his socks in the night when there's nobody there". While the rest of the song was written primarily by Paul and is credited to Lennon/McCartney, Ringo wrote that one line. Ringo did try his hand at writing, but everything he came up with was rejected by Paul and John. They treated him a little like George Harrison who had to prove himself to them as a song writer.

Ringo did, eventually get a couple songs onto albums that he wrote alone. Two of these were "Don't Pass Me By" from *The White Album* and "Octopus's Garden" from *Abbey Road*. Both of these songs are listed as written by Richard Starkey, his real name. During his years with the Beatles, these were the only two songs that they recorded that Ringo wrote. His frustration at having his writing ignored caused him to leave the group temporarily. He was only gone for two weeks before the other three convinced him to come back. He spent much of that time hanging out with the actor Peter Sellers who was a friend. They spent some time on Seller's yacht, Amelfis and it was on this yacht that he wrote "Octopus's Garden".

Ringo is credited with many other songs written during the Beatles years. On some songs like "Dig It" from the *Let It Be* album, the writing is credited to all four guys. On others, like "Flying" from the *Magical Mystery Tour* album, he shares credit with John and Paul. A few songs which we have mentioned belong to just Ringo alone. Is it any wonder that it took years to straighten out the legal questions surrounding the group after the breakup of the Beatles?

Legends of Rock & Roll – Ringo Starr (Before, During and After the Beatles)

6-THE GREATEST DRUMMER IN THE WORLD?

Just how good a drummer is Ringo Starr? Even Ringo admits that when he started he was just passable. But as he advanced with time, he became better and better. Ringo himself didn't think he was that good a drummer. He was left-handed and he played a right-handed drum kit. Because of that, he couldn't do a drum roll. But Ringo had something that not everyone has, fantastic rhythm. He could set the beat for a song.

Some say you can listen to just the drum work on a Beatles song and know what song he is playing, even without the vocals or other instruments. That is a sign of a great drummer. George Martin, their producer called Ringo "probably, the finest drummer in the world today." That is great praise from a man who knew music and was acquainted with many of the great drummers of the day.

John called Ringo underrated. Paul sent Ringo a postcard in 1969 which said "You are the greatest drummer in the world. Really" Many years later, in 2004, Ringo would publish a book called *Postcards from the Boys* in which this and fifty some other postcards from the members of the Beatles are included. This book gives a fascinating glimpse in to the minds and hearts of the individual Beatles.

Steve Smith, known as the drummer for the group Journey, said that people didn't really "see" the drummer of musical groups in the early Sixties. They could hear them, but nobody really focused on the drummer. All the attention was given to the lead singer or lead guitarist. Ringo changed all that. Suddenly people were noticing the drummer and considering him a part of the group.

James Hoag

Phil Collins, who was the drummer for the group Genesis before striking off on his own career, said he was greatly influenced by Ringo. He said that Ringo could do things that even drummers of today would have trouble doing. He said that Ringo is greatly underrated.

John Lennon said that Ringo was a star even before he joined the Beatles. He said that if Ringo would not have joined the Beatles, he would still have made a name for himself. He was on his way to greatness. "Ringo is a damn good drummer."

Ringo is known for several innovations in the drum world. He influenced other drummers to hold the sticks in a "matched grip" which means that the sticks are each held the same way. This as opposed to the traditional grip in which the sticks are each held differently. He tuned the drums lower and he had the drums placed on a riser so that they would be viable behind the other players. This was the first time that had been done.

7-THE FAMOUS BREAK-UP AND GOING SOLO

If you've read any of the other three Legends of Rock & Roll books about the members of the Beatles, you know that I don't blame the breakup of the group on Yoko Ono or Linda McCartney or any of the wives, for that matter. I think Yoko's attitude toward the guys and her influence on John was a contributing faction, but not the whole story. I believe the main reason the band broke up relates back to the death of Brian Epstein in 1967.

Epstein was the glue that held the group together and without him, they began to go their separate ways. There were certainly other factors that contributed to the breakup, nothing is black and white. Paul said that the breakup was caused by personal differences, musical differences and business differences. It did not come about over night, but was a transition that lasted over two years.

All four of the guys were working on solo albums at the time of the breakup which was officially announced by Paul McCartney to the world in November, 1969. Ringo was actually working on two albums, both of which were released in 1970. The first, *Sentimental Journey* was released on March 27, 1970. The album was a real departure from the music that the Beatles had been doing. It consists solely of standards, most from the Forties. Songs like "Night and Day" and the title song are done against a big band background. The songs were picked because they were favorites of his parents and other friends.

Strangely, I can't find any evidence that Ringo plays the drums on this album. The instrumental work is done by an in-house orchestra and

James Hoag

Ringo just sings. Based pretty much on the name Ringo Starr, the album did well, peaking at number 22 on the U.S. Album charts and at number 7 in the U.K. There were no singles from the album.

Ringo's second album was a little more of what you would expect. *Beaucoups of Blues* was released on September 25, 1970, just a few months after the first one. Ringo had met Pete Drake at a recording session for George Harrison. Drake was one of the leading Nashville based producers. He had worked with many different country singers of the Sixties including Bob Dylan's song "Lay Lady Lay" which has a country feel to it.

Ringo asked Drake if he would help him put together a country album. This was something Ringo had wanted to do his entire career. Drake agreed and told Ringo that he probably had enough material for two albums. Ringo was excited and flew to Nashville in late June, 1970 to work on the album. The result was *Beaucoups of Blues* but the album was not well received. It managed to get up to 65 in the U.S. album charts, but failed to chart in England at all. I noticed that the album has people playing on it that went on to make it big in the country world in the United States.

Charlie Daniels played guitar on the album and it was just a year or two later that he broke into the country charts in the U.S. Another was Jerry Reed who also played guitar and was just on the verge of a big career although he had been charting for a couple years already. The Jordanaires, who were the backup singers for Elvis Presley and famous in their own right, acted as backup singers for this album. That was pretty good company to be in.

Legends of Rock & Roll – Ringo Starr (Before, During and After the Beatles)

8-GETTING A LITTLE HELP FROM HIS FRIENDS

Ringo stayed kind of in the background during the actual breakup of the Beatles. So when the dust had settled he was still friends with the other three. Everyone was blaming Yoko for the breakup and Ringo had always remained friends with John and Yoko. He worked with George Harrison quite a bit. Ringo took part in the "Concert for Bangladesh" which George organized as a charity event to help the people of Bangladesh (formerly East Pakistan) after the Bhola cyclone killed more than 50,000 people.

Ringo also played drums on George's first two albums, *All Things Must Pass* and *Living in a Material World*. He played for John Lennon on *John Lennon/Plastic Ono Band* which was his first solo album after the breakup. Ringo also helped Yoko Ono on several of her earlier works. I think it is apparent that everyone liked Ringo. He had come through the breakup virtually without enemies.

Ringo was finally able to hit the single charts in his own right with a song in 1971 when he recorded "It Don't Come Easy" which at the time was not included on any album. It was just released as a single. While not his biggest hit, "It Don't Come Easy" will always be associated with Ringo Starr and has become his signature song. Ringo played drums on this record as well as lead vocals. He got his pal George Harrison to play along with him and Stephen Stills (of Crosby, Stills & Young) was on piano.

The song reached number four in the United States and England. It was number one in Canada. I suspect there were not many concerts that Ringo did over the years that did not include this song. I recently watched a broadcast of a PBS special of Ringo and his band recorded just last year (2011) and he sang "It Don't Come Easy".

A second single to be released without an album was "Back Off Boogaloo" which hit the charts in April of 1972. It's strange that this song did better in the U.K. than the previous song, peaking at number 2, but worse in the U.S., peaking at number 9. This would be the biggest hit of his solo career in the United Kingdom. This was the rare song that Ringo wrote himself. He said he was out to dinner with a friend who kept using the word "Boogaloo" in the conversation. Ringo thought the word was cool and went home to write the song.

Some people thought the song was directed at Paul McCartney. They thought the word "Boogaloo" was a nickname for Paul as he seemed to be dragging out the court battle over the Beatles royalties. Ringo was telling Paul to "back off". Sounds good to me and I probably would have believed it at the time, but years later Ringo told the story of the song and said it had nothing to do with Paul.

9-DIVERSITY

Branching out into other creative directions, Ringo directed, produced and starred in a documentary *Born to Boogie* which was about the rock group T-Rex. T-Rex was founded by Marc Bolan who was a close friend of Ringo's. The group had one hit in America, but it was a good one. "Bang a Gong (Get It On)" was Top 10 in 1972.

He found out that he liked acting and appeared in several movies over the years. Ringo appeared in such films as 200 Motels (1971), That'll Be the Day (1973), and Son of Dracula (1974). See the end of this report for a complete list.

Ringo's third album was the self-titled *Ringo*, released in November, 1973. This would be a big album for him reaching Gold in the U.K. and Platinum in the United States. It also produced three singles all of which did very well in both countries.

He and George Harrison co-wrote Ringo's next hit, "Photograph", the first single from the *Ringo* album. The song was his first number one in the United States in late 1973 and peaked at number eight in the U.K. Ringo does play the drums and sing on this song.

The second single from *Ringo* was a cover of a song from 1960. "You're Sixteen" was written by the Sherman Brothers (Robert and Richard) and was first recorded by Johnny Burnette. It hit number eight on the Billboard Top 40 in late 1960 and number three in England in 1961. Ringo's version became his second number one hit in the United States in December, 1973 and reached number four in England.

Ringo included it in the album, I think, because it has a faint country sound and Ringo liked that sound. Paul McCartney actually plays and sings on the record. About half way through the song, you hear what sounds like a kazoo and, in fact, in the liner notes of the album, Paul is credited with playing the kazoo. However, it was later revealed that Paul is not playing a kazoo; he is making those noises with his mouth, "singing" along with the record.

The third song from *Ringo* was "Oh My My" which peaked at number five in the U.S. in March of 1974, but didn't chart in England. The song was written by Ringo and Vini Poncia who would later become a producer for the band Kiss. Martha Reeves, who was the lead singer of Martha and the Vandellas and Mary Clayton sang background vocals.

It's amazing to me that all three of his mates from the Beatles contributed to this album, *Ringo*. It became Ringo's biggest album of his career.

10-GOODNIGHT VIENNA

But, no one can sit on past accomplishments, so Ringo went back to work and recorded his next album *Goodnight Vienna*. The title is English slang which means "It's all over". I don't think Ringo was talking about his career. The album rose to number eight on the U.S. album charts, but only made it to number 30 in England. Strangely enough, this would be the last Top 40 album of Ringo's career in the U.K. He would continue to chart, sometimes weakly, in the U.S., but it was pretty much over as far as England was concerned.

I love the cover for this album. It is a still shot from the 1951 science fiction movie *The Day the Earth Stood Still*. In the movie, Michael Rennie, the alien is emerging from the spaceship and waving to the people waiting for him. For the album, they pasted Ringo's face over that of Michael Rennie so it looks like Ringo is emerging from the ship. Photoshop didn't exist in those days, but they still did a pretty good job at editing the picture.

Unlike his previous album, only John played on this album. John was the one who suggested that Ringo could do a good job on the old Platters hit, "Only You (And You Alone)" This song goes back to 1955 and was the Platters first hit.

Ringo did fairly well with the song, also, peaking at number six in the United States and number 28 in the United Kingdom. One point I find interesting is that this song was number one on the U.S. Adult Contemporary chart. This was the first time Ringo had hit number on this chart, but I think it shows that the age of his listeners was getting older. Paul McCartney had hit number one on the Adult Contemporary chart that same year with "My Love", another ballad that would appeal to a older demographic.

James Hoag

"The No No Song" was also released from *Goodnight Vienna* and it did even better in the United States, peaking at number three. It was number one in Canada, but failed to chart at all in Ringo's native England. The flip side "Snookeroo" got enough air play that it charted along with "The No No Song" as a two-sided hit.

A third song from the album was sort of a title song. "It's All Down to Goodnight Vienna" was released in June, 1975. Written by his friend John Lennon, it did make the Top 40 in the U.S., peaking at number 31, but failed to chart in England. John played on the song and if you have the album, there is a reprise as the last song and right at the beginning you can hear John exclaim "OK, with gusto, boys, with gusto!" It's a cute song and I enjoy listening to it. Probably not one of Ringo's best, however.

I really like the flip side of "It's All Down to Goodnight Vienna" which is called "Oo-Wee". Check it out on YouTube if you have time. Like other records, it got enough air play to qualify as a two-sided record on the charts. The significant thing about "Oo-Wee" is that Dr. John plays the piano on the record. The solo in the middle of the song is very cool. I think you'll enjoy it.

11-BLAST FROM YOUR PAST

At this point, Ringo and his team felt that they had enough material released to put out a Greatest Hits album. *Blast From Your Past*, which was released in 1975, was a ten-song compilation that included every hit he had had up until that time. The album, released late in 1975, managed to get to number 30 in the United States, but, once again did not chart in the U.K. This would be his last album on the Apple label.

By the end of 1975, Ringo had moved to Monte Carlo for tax purposes. This was the same reason John Lennon moved to the United States in the Seventies. Ringo also had a house in Los Angeles. His girlfriend of the year was Nancy Andrews, whom he started dating. Andrews was an American model who turned photographer and specialized in pictures of rock artists. She and Ringo actually got engaged, but it didn't last. After the breakup, Andrews sued Ringo for palimony.

Not one to stay off the horse for long, Ringo found a new girlfriend, Lynsey De Paul who is called England's first successful singer-songwriter. Ringo helped her out when he could.

Ringo's star was starting to fade a little. He signed on with Atlantic Records in the United States and with Polydor in England after his contract with Apple expired and set about to record his next album, *Ringo's Rotogravure*. The album made number 28 in the U.S, but did not chart in the U.K.

The only single that charted in the Top 40 from *Rotogravure* was "A Dose of Rock and Roll" which is a fun song and peaked at number 26 in the U.S. A second single was released from the album. This one,

"Hey Baby" was a cover (pretty much note for note) of a number song from 1961 by Bruce Channel. The song did not make the Top 40, peaking at number 74.

Forging on, Ringo next released *Ringo the 4th* in 1978. In the past, Ringo had used his friends to write the material or play on the song. This time, he and Vini Poncia pretty much did it all and they used session musicians. The album was a disaster, not receiving any love from the critics or from the public. The name is odd since this was Ringo's sixth solo album but Ringo explained that this was his forth "rock" album. At any rate, it sank quickly out of sight.

When artists fail commercially, they quite often blame it on the label, so Ringo changed labels again and this time signed with Portrait Records. (Actually Atlantic dropped him, as did Polydor in the U.K.) His first album with Portrait looked like it should be a winner. Called *Bad Boy*, they even developed a television special based around the album to encourage sales. But it was all for naught. The album did only a little better than "the 4th", peaking at number 129 in the U.S. This was the one only album Ringo recorded for Portrait.

I like the title song, however. But, I have always been a fan of Doo Wop from the Fifties. *Bad Boy* was originally done by a group called The Jive Bombers in 1957. It barely made the Top 40, peaking at number 36 for one lonely week. But, the song is a classic to those of us who love Doo Wop. Ringo's version does not live up to the original, but he gave it a good effort. Also, don't get confused by the song with the same title that the Beatles did. Their *Bad Boy* is a completely different song. The Beatles version is a cover of 1958 Larry Williams song. I actually like the Williams version better. It seems more genuine.

Legends of Rock & Roll – Ringo Starr (Before, During and After the Beatles)

12-RING O'RECORDS

Ringo decided that it was time to form his own label. That way he had complete control over the recording and, really, no one to blame for the failures. Ring O'Records was created in 1975 and signed a few other performers to record for the new label. I think Ringo intended to record his own music on this new label, but I can't find any evidence that he did. The very first album produced by Ring O'Records was a Ringo album of sorts. It was called *Sta*rtling Music*. The artist is David Hentschel who created a re-make of the original *Ringo* album, only this is completely instrumental, with Hentschel playing the synthesizer. Ringo does play on the album, but no vocals. As far as I can tell, it's the only Ring O'Records album released in the United States.

But, Ringo wasn't a business man. He didn't like going to meetings and he didn't like worrying about contracts and all the other legal work that a record producer has to worry about. The company limped along for a few more years and then quietly folded. Ringo had lost interest and gone on to other things.

1979 turned out to be a rough year for Ringo. Never very healthy, in April, he collapsed from intestinal problems that was related to his bout with peritonitis as a child. The surgeons had to remove several feet of intestine. Recovering from that, in November, his Los Angeles home burned to the ground and Ringo lost most of his Beatles memorabilia. It was a touch year.

Ringo liked to act and later he did several commercials for various companies. In 1980, he got the lead role in the movie *Caveman* which is a silly comedy which is supposed to take place "1 Zillion B.C.". The film also stars Dennis Quaid, Shelly Long and Barbara Bach.

James Hoag

Ringo played Atouk who was scrawny and picked on by the bigger cavemen. He secretly liked Lana (played by Bach) but Lana is the mate of Tonda who is big and strong. Tonda doesn't like Atouk hanging around his girl, so he kicks him out of the tribe and Atouk is on his own (with a couple friends played by Quaid and Long). It's a silly movie. The visitors at IMDB.Com give it 5.4 stars out of 10 which makes it about average.

13-BARBARA BACH

The key factor coming out of this film was that Ringo and Barbara Bach did get together, even if it wasn't in the movie. Barbara is American, born Barbara Goldbach in Rosedale, Queens, New York on August 27, 1947. She left school to become a model and transitioned to being an actress in the Sixties. She has 28 films to her credit, but probably her most famous role was as a "Bond Girl" in the James Bond movie *The Spy Who Loved Me*. Ringo proposed and Barbara and he were married on April 27, 1981. George and Olivia Harrison and Paul and Linda McCartney attended the ceremony. Barbara brought two children into the marriage from a previous marriage but her and Ringo have never had any children. Barbara has toured with Ringo over the years and they are still married to this day.

In 1980, George Harrison wrote a song "All Those Years Ago" which was meant for Ringo. He was going to use it in his next album which was eventually called *Stop and Smell the Roses*, but John Lennon was killed on December 8, 1980 and George pulled back the song. He then re-wrote it as a tribute to John and included it on his *Somewhere in England* album. On December 9th, Ringo and Barbara flew to New York to comfort Yoko Ono.

Stop and Smell the Roses was Ringo's 8th studio album and was a who's who of performers working on it. George Harrison did contribute a song to the album called "Wrack My Brain" which would be the last single that Ringo charted on the American charts. It peaked at number 38 in late 1981. George also produced several of the songs on the album.

Other notables associated with the album were Paul McCartney, Eric Clapton, Ron Woods (of the Rolling Stones) and Harry Nilsson, all of which played on songs and/or produced them for Ringo. *Stop and Smell the Roses* would be Ringo's bestselling album since *Goodnight Vienna*, back in 1974. However, it only reached number 98 on the U.S. charts and did not chart at all in England.

John Lennon had written two songs for Ringo to include on "Roses", "Nobody Told Me" and "Life Begins at 40", but after John's death, Ringo didn't feel right about recording them and they were left off. After Lennon's death, Ringo did not feel safe in the United States and moved back to Tittenhurst Park which he had purchased from John and Yoko in 1973 and was his home until the mid-Eighties. Tittenhurst Park, a 26 room mansion sits on a 72 acre estate near Ascot in the U.K. John had built a recording studio in the house which he called "Ascot Studios". When Ringo took over, he renamed the studio "Startling Studios"

14-INTO THE EIGHTIES

Feeling that maybe too many cooks spoil the broth, Ringo opted to work with just one man on his next album. He had been friends with Joe Walsh, formerly of the Eagles and asked him to produce the new album. Originally called *It Beats Sleep*, the album came out in June, 1983 as *Old Wave*. Looking at the album cover, Ringo does not look happy. The cover just displays a head shot of him staring straight at the camera, with no smile, not much of an expression at all.

There were no hits from the album, but one song that stands out for me is "I Keep Forgetting" which is an old Jerry Leiber/Mike Stoller song which was recorded in 1962 by Chuck Jackson. I love almost anything by Leiber/Stoller. Ringo's contract with RCA had expired and he was in the embarrassing position of having to find a record label when no one really wanted him.

Old Wave was not the hit Ringo was looking for. He couldn't find a label to distribute it in England or the United States. He finally convinced RCA/Canada to distribute it in a few counties, but not the U.S. or England. That is probably why it didn't chart in either country or anywhere else, for that matter. I'm sure Ringo was discouraged because he did not record another album for nine years.

From 1984 until 1986, Ringo decided to diversify a little. He had already done some acting, so he was asked to be the narrator for "Thomas the Tank Engine & Friends", a live action model animation show which was broadcast on British television starting in 1984. It still runs today, however, Ringo was involved only during the first and second series. He also played the character "Mr. Conductor" in a spin off series which was shown on PBS in the United States called "Shining Time Station".

James Hoag

Not recording gives you time to do other things. Ringo participated in the "Artists United Against Apartheid" concert in 1985 and played on the song "Sun City" which was recorded as a protest song. "Artists United Against Apartheid" was organized by Stephen Van Zandt who played with the E-Street Band with Bruce Springsteen. He still does today.

A couple years later, in 1987, George Harrison recorded "When We Was Fab" for his *Cloud Nine* album and Ringo played drums on that song. Later in the year, he participated with many great English performers for the Prince's Trust Rock Concert in 1987. Prince Charles and Princess Diana attended the concert which featured such performers as George Harrison, Elton John, Eric Clapton, Phil Collins and others; and, Ringo, of course.

15-Ringo Starr and His All-Starr Band

In 1988, Ringo and his wife Barbara Bach voluntarily entered into an alcohol treatment clinic in Tucson, Arizona. They both recognized that they had an alcohol problem. The treatment lasted 6-weeks. Once Ringo was sober, he felt like going back to work doing what he does best, recording and performing.

In 1989, Ringo organized what was to be the first of several different variations of his "All-Starr Band". In the band everyone was a "star" in their own right. When the band performed, no matter who was in it, Ringo would sing his songs and include some Beatles songs and then the individual members would do songs that they had made famous.

The very first "All-Starr Band" consisted of Joe Walsh(of Eagles fame), Nils Lofgren and Clarence Clemons (who played with Bruce Springsteen in the E-Street Band), Rick Danko and Levon Helm (from The Band) as well as Dr John, Billy Preston and Jim Kelter

There have been twelve incarnations of the "All-Starr Band" as of this writing and it continues to this day. Each variation has new people and some leave for a while and then come back in a later version. Others leave and never come back. Besides those already mentioned, Ringo has played with such "stars" as Todd Rundgren, Dave Edmunds, Randy Bachman (Bachman-Turner Overdrive), Peter Frampton, Eric Carmen, Howard Jones, Colin Hay (Men at Work), Sheila E., Edgar Winter and Gary Wright. These are just some of the names that I recognize. There were many more performers who at one time or another played with Ringo Starr.

James Hoag

The first group was so successful on the road that they decided to release an album of live performances. If you check the list of albums at the end of this report, you'll see that *Ringo Starr and His All-Starr Band* was his first live album. The album contains 12 songs, about half of which are Ringo Starr hits from the past. The others are covers like the Buddy Holly song "Raining In My Heart" or songs made famous by members of the band, like "The Weight", performed by Rick Danko and Levon Helm (from The Band). While the shows were well received and the critics liked the live album, unfortunately, it failed to chart in the United States.

In 1989, Ringo got together with country singer Buck Owens and the two did a duet of "Act Naturally". To my knowledge, this is the only time Ringo appears on the Country charts. "Act Naturally" was originally done by Buck Owens and was a number one country song in 1963. Two years later, the Beatles recorded it with Ringo singing lead vocal. It didn't make the Top 40 (#47), but everyone who is a Beatles fan knows the song. The 1989 duet also made the Country chart peaking at number 27. A fun song and a fun video which combines two genres.

16-Fun with the Simpsons

Ringo still liked to do voice-overs in cartoons and in 1991, appeared as himself in an episode of the Simpsons on Fox-TV. This was during the second season of the show and was entitled "Brush With Greatness". It seems when Marge Simpson was in high school, she painted several pictures of Ringo and sent him one. But, he never replied. Now, many years later, Ringo has gotten though his stack of fan mail and replies to Marge praising the picture.

Ringo is the first of the Beatles to appear on the Simpsons. Later, both Paul and George would make guest appearances (Paul appeared twice), but, of course John never did as he had died before the Simpsons even aired.

1992 saw the release of his next studio album *Time Takes Time*. This was called his comeback album because he hadn't recorded a studio album in nine years. The album was critically acclaimed but largely ignored by the public. The album did not chart except in Australia and Sweden, of all places. My favorite song on the album is a cover of the old Elvis Presley classic "Don't Be Cruel". I can't say he does as good a job as Elvis, but it's a rocker and I enjoyed listening to it.

1994 was another bad year for Ringo. In January, his friend, Harry Nilsson, who had played and sang on several of Ringo's albums, died of a heart attack. In August, his stepfather, Harry Graves, who Ringo had always been close to, died of pneumonia. Then, in December, his first wife Maureen died from complications due to leukemia.

In 1995, Ringo appeared in a Pizza Hut commercial which I actually remember. In the commercial, he is with Micky Dolenz, Davy Jones and Peter Tork of the Monkees. I think this was during the period

James Hoag

when Michael Nesmith wouldn't have anything to do with the group. Ringo's job, in the commercial, talks about getting his boys back together again. (Not to play, but to eat pizza) In the end, the Monkees join Ringo, but as the commercial ends, Ringo turns to the camera and says "Wrong lads". A classic that you can view today on YouTube.

While not as successful as the other Beatles had been, Ringo was having a good time. He worked with Paul and George on *The Beatles Anthology*, a set of three double albums and documentation that chronicled the history of the Beatles. This opened up the Beatles to a whole new generation and people were talking about him and the other guys again.

He played on Paul McCartney's album *Flaming Pie* which came out in 1997. He co-wrote a song for the album with Paul called "Really Love You" which became the first time a song was written by McCartney/Starkey. Switching labels with almost every album, he joined Mercury Records and in 1998, released *Vertical Man* which put him back on the charts, although not that high. *Vertical Man* got to 61 in the United States and 85 in England. While not a smash, it is the best he had done since 1976 with *Rotograveur*.

17-THE TWENTY-FIRST CENTURY

Vertical Man would be the last appearance of George Harrison on a Ringo album. George would die of lung cancer in 2001. Following Ringo's style of bringing in famous names to be his band, several big names appeared on *Vertical Man* besides George. Paul McCartney took part as well as Brian Wilson of the Beach Boys, Alanis Morissette, Ozzy Osbourne, Tom Petty and others.

Another album recorded on the Mercury label came out the same year. This one was a recording of the television program *VH1 Storytellers* which features Ringo and Joe Walsh. The show aired on VH1 in 1998 and the album was released shortly after. It contains mostly Beatles and Ringo Starr songs with Ringo describing how each song came to be written, sort of a backstory album. While the song received some critical acclaim, it did not chart. I find it interesting that this is the first Ringo album to be released on a pre-recorded cassette. In 1998, the death of the cassette was already being predicted by most people as the CD took over the music industry. Why they would start producing cassettes at this late date is a mystery to me.

On November 29, 2002, the one year anniversary of the death of George Harrison was celebrated with the famous "Concert for George". Of course Ringo took part singing "Photograph" and a rendition of an old Carl Perkins song, "Honey Don't" According to people in the audience, Ringo literally brought a tear to their eye when he sang "Photograph" as it had been one song that he and George had written together. The line that brought tears was "But all I've got is a photograph / and I realize you're not coming back anymore"

Every year NORAD holds an event on Christmas Eve in which they track Santa as his sleigh full of presents makes its way around the world. During the 2003 and 2004 seasons, NORAD hired Ringo to be the voice of NORAD and describe the journey of Santa. According to NORAD, Ringo was a "Starr in the East" that helped carry on the tradition of Santa's flight.

Still recording an album every couple years or so, in 2003, he released *Ringo Rama* on yet another label, Koch Records. It was a similar album to *Vertical Man* with lots of famous stars with every single song co-written by Ringo. The critics liked it, but the album only peaked at number 113 in the U.S. and didn't chart in England at all.

In an interesting turn of events, the Liverpool City Council decided to tear down the home where Ringo lived the first three years of his life, 9 Madyrn Street in Liverpool. They said it didn't have any historical value. Well, the people of Liverpool had other ideas and protested. The City Council finally decided to take the house apart, brick by brick and move it somewhere else so it could be preserved.

In 2006, he performed with Jerry Lee Lewis on his duet album *Last Man Standing*, an album I own and recommend very highly. He sang the Chuck Berry hit "Sweet Little Sixteen" with Lewis.

Legends of Rock & Roll – Ringo Starr (Before, During and After the Beatles)

18-LIVERPOOL 8

Moving along, *Liverpool 8*, his 14th studio album, was released in 2008. It marks his return to the EMI label which he recorded for right after the Beatles breakup. The title refers to the postal code where Ringo was born. I'm assuming it's sort of like a zip code. The album did fairly well, being the first of his in 10 years to chart in England where it reached number 91. It also cracked the Top 100 in the United States, reaching number 94. *Liverpool 8* was the first time he worked with Dave Stewart as a producer. Stewart is half of the English group, The Eurythmics.

Mark Hudson had been Ringo's producer and co-writer for several albums, but with *Liverpool 8*, they went their separate ways. Hudson later said it was because Ringo wanted to use synthesized music on the album instead of old-fashioned guitars and pianos.

On October 10, 2008, Ringo posted on his website that he would no longer provide autographs to fans. So, if you have one, hang onto it, it's probably valuable. He said he was just too busy to do it anymore.

It's great to be busy. In 2009, he joined with Paul McCartney for the "Change Begins Within" Benefit Concert at Radio City Music. No one knew that he was there and when it came time for Paul to play his set, he introduced "Billy Shears" to come out and help him. Out walked Ringo to the delight of the audience. They did "With a Little Help From My Friends" and then brought out all of the performers of the concert and did "I Saw Her Standing There". Truly a magical night.

Also, in 2009, he returned to his role as the voice of "Thomas the Tank Engine" cartoon. He performed in a single called "The Official BBC

Children in Need Medley". This single did go to number one in England selling over 400,000 copies. We don't count this as a number one song for Ringo since he only played a small part in the song. The cover of the single shows many of the characters from children's TV and is a parody of the Sgt. Peppers album cover by the Beatles.

In 2010, he released his 15th studio album, *Y Not*. To promote it, he ran the late night circuit, appearing on *The Tonight Show* with Jay Leno and *Late Night* with Jimmy Fallon and *The Daily Show* with Jon Stewart. He appeared on many other programs both here in the States and in the U.K. It paid off because the album debuted at number 58 on the Billboard Hot 200 Album chart. This was the highest debut of any Ringo Starr album since 1976. Unfortunately, that's as high as it got, dropping completely off the chart two weeks later.

The last album Ringo has released, as of this writing, was *Ringo 2012* which was released in January of this year (2012). It has, so far, peaked at number 80 in the United States and number 181 in the U.K. But, Ringo is still going strong. He plays frequently and is still recording and there's a good chance you will be able to see him in the future. I watched a special on some cable channel just a couple weeks ago which featured him and the latest incarnation of the "All-Starr Band" and I enjoyed it very much.

Ringo has done pretty well for himself. In 2011, he was listed as the 56th wealthiest person in England with a personal wealth of about £150 Million. He and wife Barbara own three homes in Cranleigh, Surrey, England, Los Angeles, California and Monte Carlo.

19-Legacy of Ringo Starr

In 1965, along with the other three members of the Beatles, he was awarded the "Member of the Order of the British Empire" (MBE). They received their medals directly from the Queen herself.

All four of the Beatles have had minor planets named after them. Ringo's was number 4150 and is now called "Starr"

In 1989, Ringo was nominated for a Daytime Emmy for *Outstanding Performer in a Children's Series* for playing Mr. Conductor in "Shining Time Station"

The Beatles were inducted into the *Rock and Roll Hall of Fame* in 1988 and since then the other three, John, Paul and George have individually been inducted into the Hall of Fame. However, Ringo is the only one of the Fab Four who has not been inducted. There are several petitions online to try to correct this oversight, but no results yet.

Ringo received a Grammy award in 2008 at the 50th Grammy Awards for *Best Compilation Soundtrack* for the compilation album of Beatles music, *Love* that was released in 2006. He shared that award with George Martin and Giles Martin.

Also, in 2008, he accepted a Chopard Diamond Award in behalf of the other Beatles at the World Music Awards in Monaco. The award is given to musical performers who have sold over 100 million albums over the course of their career.

In 2002, Ringo was inducted into the Percussive Arts Hall of Fame, an organization that honors drummers and others that are in the percussion field. Other inductees are Buddy Rich and Gene Krupa. Nice company to be in.

Ringo got his star in the Hollywood Walk of Fame in February of 2010. It is located in front of the Capitol Records Building and is near the stars for John, Paul and George. It was the 2401st star awarded.

AFTERWORD

Ringo hit number one in the United States, twice, but he is the only one of the four Beatles to never have a number one in England. Very curious to me. It reminds me of the scripture that a prophet is never honored in his own country. I'm not saying that Ringo is a prophet, but he was a member of the greatest rock group in history, yet that doesn't seem to be recognized in his native country, England.

It is agreed by everyone I read to put together this report, that the Beatles would not have been the same without Ringo. They probably would still have been famous. They might have kept Pete Best and he could have gone on to be their drummer. However, replacing him with Ringo took a vision that not everyone has. Brian Epstein and George Martin saw that vision and brought in Ringo. I'm so glad they did.

Ringo turned 72 this year (2012). You would never know it. The last time I saw him on television, he rocked and sang like a man 20 years younger. I enjoy the music of all the Beatles, but Ringo has always held a special place in my heart. He seemed like the underdog to me. He never got as much attention as the others and I can relate to that. I will remain a fan as long as he keeps performing.

You can contact me at www.number1project.com where I occasionally blog about things that interest me in the music world (mostly, the twentieth century). Go find it and read it and leave me a comment. I also have a Facebook fan page called "Legends of Rock & Roll". "Like" me and comment there, too. If you love the music as much as I do, you'll enjoy the trip. Thanks for reading.

I hope you have enjoyed this book as much as I have enjoyed writing it for you.

James Hoag

If you have liked what you read, will you please do me a favor and leave a review of "Ringo Starr". Thank you.

About the Author

James Hoag has always been a big fan of Rock & Roll. Most people graduate from high school and then proceed to "grow up" and go on to more adult types of music. James got stuck at about age 18 and has been an avid fan of popular music ever since. His favorite music is from the Fifties, the origin of Rock & Roll and which was the era in which James grew up. But he likes almost all types of popular music including country music.

In 1980, he became friends with a man who introduced him to Country Music and he has been a strong fan of that genre of music ever since.

After working his entire life as a computer programmer, he is now retired, and he decided to share his love of the music and of the performers by writing books that discuss the life and music of the various people who have meant so much to him over the years.

He calls each book a "love letter" to the stars that have enriched our lives so much. These people are truly Legends.

FILMS

A Hard Day's Night (1964)

Help! (1965)

Magical Mystery Tour (1967)

Yellow Submarine (1968)

Candy (1968)

The Magic Christian (1969)

Let It Be (1970)

Blindman (1971)

Frank Zappa's 200 Motels (1971)

The Point (1971)

Born to Boogie (1972)

That'll Be the Day (1973)

Son of Dracula (1974)

Lisztomania (1975)

Sextette (1978)

The Last Waltz (1978)

Ringo (1978)

The Kids Are Alright (1979)

Legends of Rock & Roll – Ringo Starr (Before, During and After the Beatles)

Caveman (1981)

The Compleat Beatles (1982)

Princess Daisy (1983)

Give My Regards to Broad Street (1984)

Water (1985)

The Return of Bruno (1988)

The Beatles Anthology (1995)

Goat Boy (1996)

The Cooler (2003)

James Hoag

SELECTED DISCOGRAPHY

STUDIO ALBUMS

1970 Sentimental Journey (Apple)

1970 Beaucoups of Blues (Apple)

1973 Ringo (Apple)

1974 Goodnight Vienna (Apple)

1976 Ringo's Rotogravure (Atlantic)

1977 Ringo the 4th (Atlantic)

1978 Bad Boy (Portrait)

1981 Stop and Smell the Roses (RCA)

1983 Old Wave (RCA)

1992 Time Takes Time (Private Music)

1998 Vertical Man (Mercury)

2003 Ringo Rama (Koch)

2005 Choose Love (Koch)

2008 Liverpool 8 (EMI, Capitol)

2010 Y Not (Hip-O)

2012 Ringo 2012 (Hip-O)

Legends of Rock & Roll – Ringo Starr (Before, During and After the Beatles)

LIVE ALBUMS

1990 Ringo Starr and His All-Starr Band (Rykodisc)

1993 Ringo Starr and His All Starr Band Volume 2: Live from Montreux (Rykodisc)

1997 Ringo Starr and His Third All-Starr Band-Volume 1 (Blockbuster)

1998 VH1 Storytellers (Mercury)

2002 King Biscuit Flower Hour Presents Ringo & His New All-Starr Band (King Biscuit)

2003 Extended Versions (BMG)

2004 Tour 2003 (Koch)

2006 Ringo Starr and Friends (Disky)

2007 Ringo Starr: Live at Soundstage (Koch)

2008 Ringo Starr & His All Starr Band Live 2006 (Koch)

2010 Live at the Greek Theatre 2008 (Universal Music)

SINGLES

1970 "Beaucoups of Blues"

1971 "It Don't Come Easy"

1972 "Back Off Boogaloo"

1973 "Photograph"

1973 "You're Sixteen"

James Hoag

1974 "Oh My My"

1974 "Only You (And You Alone)"

1975 "No No Song"/"Snookeroo"

1975 "It's All Down to Goodnight Vienna"/"Oo-Wee"

1976 "A Dose of Rock 'n' Roll"

1976 "Hey! Baby"

1977 "Wings"

1977 "Drowning in the Sea of Love"

1978 "Lipstick (On a Cigarette)"

1978 "Heart on My Sleeve"

1981 "Wrack My Brain"

1982 "Private Property"

1992 "Weight of the World"

1998 "La De Da"

1999 "Come On Christmas, Christmas Come On"

2003 "Never Without You"

2005 "Fading In and Fading Out"

2008 "Liverpool 8"

2009 "The Official BBC Children in Need Medley"

2009 "Walk with You" (with Paul McCartney)

2012 "Wings"

Legends of Rock & Roll – Ringo Starr (Before, During and After the Beatles)

CPSIA information can be obtained
at www.ICGtesting.com
Printed in the USA
LVHW051752080321
680889LV00042B/3053

9 781087 257082